ABSOLUTE PROSPERITY

My Divine Heritage

Dr. Christine A. McLean, Msc.D

Trafford
PUBLISHING

Order this book online at www.trafford.com/07-1438
or email orders@trafford.com

Most Trafford titles are also available at major online book retailers.

Note for Librarians: A cataloguing record for this book is available from Library
and Archives Canada at www.collectionscanada.ca/amicus/index-e.html

ISBN: 978-1-4251-3664-2

*We at Trafford believe that it is the responsibility of us all, as both individuals
and corporations, to make choices that are environmentally and socially sound.
You, in turn, are supporting this responsible conduct each time you purchase a
Trafford book, or make use of our publishing services. To find out how you are
helping, please visit www.trafford.com/responsiblepublishing.html*

*Our mission is to efficiently provide the world's finest, most comprehensive
book publishing service, enabling every author to experience success.
To find out how to publish your book, your way, and have it available
worldwide, visit us online at www.trafford.com/10510*

🌊 **Trafford**
PUBLISHING™

www.trafford.com

North America & international
toll-free: 1 888 232 4444 (USA & Canada)
phone: 250 383 6864 ♦ fax: 250 383 6804
email: info@trafford.com

The United Kingdom & Europe
phone: +44 (0)1865 722 113 ♦ local rate: 0845 230 9601
facsimile: +44 (0)1865 722 868 ♦ email: info.uk@trafford.com

10 9 8 7 6 5

Please share your thoughts and experiences with me.

I am also available to you for spiritual consultation and coaching.

Please feel free to contact me at the e -mail address below:

E-MAIL: Dr.Mc808@gmail.com

Coming soon: Advanced techniques used by the masters, to further intensify your inherent powers.

These things are necessary to make everyone great:

1. Conviction of the powers of Goodness.

2. Absence of jealousy and suspicion.

3. Helping all who are trying to be and do good.

Swami Vivekananda
Letters of Swami Vivekananda

God does respond when you deeply pray to him with faith and dedication... You don't realize how wonderful this great power works. It is mathematically proven. There is no "IF" about it.

Paramhansa Yoganda
Founder, Self Realization Fellowship

The most interesting phenomena are, of course, in the new places.

The old rules do not work in the places where they did work!

This is the way in which we discover new rules.

Richard Feynman
Physicist, Nobel Laureate

To the Reader

This inspired book is the result of years of observation and pondering the plight of lack of peace in and about humanity, in specific, the lack of Absolute Prosperity in and about myself, and the lives of so many of us.

In 1993, I was introduced to the idea of me as being a Divine Soul, and that the soul of a human being contained all the infinite knowledge and power that there is in the Universe.

Shortly after embracing these ideas, I started to meditate daily and found that my life quickly improved. Some of the first and most engaging memories of these changes I noticed, were that I felt more peaceful immediately after my first meditation and my perception of self and others quickly changed. I became happier and enjoyed much more love and kindness from others. I now look forward to each day of my life and welcome the experience that each day brings.

In the beginning of 1994, I realize one of my desires. I started a business with no money. This was achieved through a series of events that I can only describe as being mystical. In 1995, the opportunity came for me to advance my business to an international status.

I had $400 to invest in products, and in the new country, I setup business. I purchased $387.00 worth of products and turned that initial investment into just over $250,000 in sales, in less than 3 years.

I needed to understand how I achieved all this in such a short period of time, so I embarked on the study of Metaphysical Science. During the research of a Masters Thesis, it became clear to me that the perception of a human being was the total sum of one's life reality.

Prior to embarking on the path of living in the focused consciousness, I struggled for many years pondering why I felt so much lack in and about myself, and why the same was true for countless other human beings. This is true in spite of dreams, desires and all of the hard work that we do.

On the morning of December 21, 2005, after meditation, the information that is contained in these pages came flooding into the forefront of my mind. I felt compelled to write it. At first, I wrote it for myself; then, concluded that, as I am a link in the chain of the Divine Goodness that is intended for all of us. **I needed to share it with you.**

Please read each chapter until you feel at peace with its contents before reading the others. Your doing so, will enable you to better benefit from them.

It is my sole intent to share with you what know and believe to be the TRUTH. It is your choice how, where and when you create for yourself whatever it is that you desire to be your life's reality.

Cultures, religions and ethnic diversity sometimes limit our languages, thoughts and beliefs. Please feel free to substitute whatever name that is, that you feel comfortable with for The Divine, God, Source, and the Almighty Creator.

You too can realize Absolute Prosperity in and about you.

TABLE OF CONTENTS

ACKNOWLEDGEMENT

A special thank you to Dr. Paul Masters of the University of Metaphysics and The University of Sedona for his clear and concise and enlightened teachings.

To My Parents: Beresford and Marion McLean it is good that you procured and nurtured my existence. Thank you.

To My Sister: Rev. Marion Lowe Mc Lean, thank you for exposing me to the truth of my being.

To My Brothers: Trevor, Beresford, Basil and Cleveland Mc Lean, thank you for your support, your kindness, and challenges that you hurled at me. The good thing is that I have grown.

To The Editor: RoseLyn O'Laughlin Small. Thank you for sharing your genius. Your lighthearted approach to the task was inspiring and greatly appreciated.

PART 1

ABSOLUTE PROSPERITY IS MY DIVINE HERITAGE

CHAPTER 1
ABSOLUTE PROSPERITY IS MY DIVINE HERITAGE

By absolute prosperity I mean a state in which one is, and feels, a oneness with the Divine that expresses perfect health, wealth, happiness, wisdom, love, true contentment, and peace within and about one's self.

It is my intent to share with you THE TRUTH that will show you a way of living that can bring more love, wealth, successes, peace, happiness, fulfillment, creativity and awareness into your life. WELCOME!

You are about to discover how to use "your inherent powers," the "same powers" that Christ and many others used down through the ages to which so-called Supernatural power was attributed.

We need not look very far to see that this is possible. Take a look at Oprah Winfrey. In spite of her humble beginnings, compounded by sexual abuse, ridicule, and racism that she endured as a child, and perhaps still endures, she has become a "self-made Billionaire" in about 25 years, in spite of all the odds stacked up against her. She did not accomplish this by coincidence.

She "turned the other cheek"; found her true identity and purpose, and now lives each day of her life in the consciousness of focused intent to create what she desires to be her life's reality.

"Rich" means having an abundance of good, or living a fuller more satisfying life.

You have within you the honorable methods through which, you can quickly realize your goals.

You can solve your own economic and personal troubles and create for yourself the prosperous life that is rightfully yours.

Lack of prosperity in and about you is filthy; it is a form of hell that causes one to be blind to the Divine Unlimited Good that exists in and about oneself.

Absolute Prosperity is our Divine Heritage. The Bible tells us that, as a child of our Divine Creator, we are intended to be Absolutely Prosperous. That we share in and enjoy all of the abundance and goodness that was created in and around us.

Make no mistake about it! Absolute Prosperity is our divine heritage!

So why are you not accepting your divine inheritance of absolute prosperity?

We cannot keep making excuses for putting up with lack of, or be accepting of it, as a permanent part of your existence.

You are and will be prosperous to the degree of your expectancy.

Understand this, you need to accept your inheritance of Absolute Prosperity from your Divine Creator in order to live a prosperous life.

You cannot, and will not be useful to yourself or anyone else living in a deprived state.

So then, take a bold and deliberate step to eradicate lack of, from within and about yourself.

Oprah Winfrey, Bill Gates, Nelson Mandela's and many other success stories that we hear and read about, were created Human Beings just like you.

They walk, talk, eat, and sleep just like you. They even breathe the same air as you do.

What sets them apart is that they are able to create for themselves, the life reality that they desire. And so can you!

These celebrities do so by living their lives in a state of being consciously or unconsciously synchronized with, and connected to the Universal Intelligence or God Mind.

With focused intent, guided by the Divine, they are able to manifest their desires, to become their life's reality.

Most human beings have developed a pattern of living in which we become comfortable and complacent. This state of stagnation enables us to become resistant to change, and in most cases, causes us to be unwilling to accept change.

It is only through the spiritual awakening, to our true identity, that we become empowered to rid ourselves of this inertia, and become able to create for ourselves a life of wholeness and "Absolute Prosperity".

Your belief and faith, in the Divine Universal Intelligence, that is embedded within you, combined with your willingness to take action and create change, are all that is needed to bring about absolute change and complete Prosperity in your life.

This process is no mystery, or the right of passage for some. It is your inherent right to be absolutely prosperous.

The sole intent of our forgiving, loving, kind and generous Creator is that we are to be Absolutely Prosperous and feel completely contented.

You must accept, your true identity, as being a "Divine Soul" with infinite power and possibilities and live each day of your life in that consciousness.

Use your inherent, proven, Divine powers to achieve all that you can imagine and desire to be your life's reality.

There is a remarkable union with our body, our mind and our spirit. Which when synchronized with the Collective Universal Intelligence produces harmony and prosperity within and around us.

We must live every moment of our lives in confident assurance that the Divine Will and POWER within us, permit us to manifest into reality all of the GOOD that we want to manifest into reality for ourselves.

Understand fully, and be completely convinced, that absolute prosperity is the only true Divine Will and intent of our Creator for all of us.

Some of us pray, unceasingly, to a Higher Power, to perform Miracles in our lives, then wonder, where are the miracles that they pray for?

We pray because we believe that there is a higher power that performs Miracles in their lives. Then why are we not demonstrating them?

It is not necessary to pray for the same thing unceasingly. The Source of miracles that you pray to is not deaf. It is your belief and faith in the INFINITE DIVINE power within you, to co-create with your Creator; whatever it is that you desire, combined with your thoughts, deeds and actions that will manifest what it is that you truly desire. This makes all the difference.

It is not enough to desire and ask for things. You must take action in confident assurance and consciousness, that you must have them, and you will have them. It is the desire of our loving kind and forgiving Creator to co-create with, and through you all of the good, that you desire for yourself.

Think about this:

I know nothing if I cannot manifest and demonstrate for myself a good life.

PART 2

ME
THE SOULFUL REALITY

CHAPTER 2
Me The Soulful Reality

You are a <u>Human Being.</u> The most recent definition found is "A DIVINE" (<u>Webster's Dictionary 2005</u>.)

"A DIVINE" means belonging to or having the nature of your Creator. (Webster's Dictionary 2005)

You are much greater than a name, ethnicity, physical appearance, or profession. These are all labels and roles that we play in our day-to-day existence.

The Almighty Creator said let us make human beings into our own image, and so He/She formed us from the dust of the ground, and breathed into our nostrils the breath of life; and we became living "Souls."

I am a soul made in the image and likeness of my Divine Creator, and I am filled with all of the infinite knowledge, powers and possibilities of my Creator, that which I can use to achieve whatever it is that I desire to be my life's reality.

Absolute Prosperity in and about me is most definitely my Divine heritage. I am a child of my Absolutely Prosperous Creator. The source of all GOOD, and it is absolutely natural and normal that I inherit the Spiritual Anatomy, and Biological Genes of my Creator.

AND SO I DECLARE:

I AM A SOUL. I AM A SOUL. I AM A SOUL. I AM THAT WHICH I AM, AN INFINITELY WISE, POWER-FUL, CREATIVE, KIND, LOV-ING AND ABSOLUTELY PROS-PEROUS SOUL. FOR THIS I GIVE THANKS

THAT IT IS SO. AND SO IT IS!

A Shocking Discovery

A shocking discovery that I made, was that most Human Beings feel guilty, and not deserving of power and riches, even though they desire them, and work very hard to achieve riches every day of their lives. Some were even business people.

In my quest for the cause of their guilty feeling, I discovered that they believed that being wealthy was not spiritual, and that wealth would hinder their souls from going to heaven. Their thoughts and desires created conflict in their thinking.

This was, in turn, transferred to their affairs, and served to neutralize their efforts to succeed, despite their hard work.

The Creator, Human Beings and Prosperity are divinely related.

Poverty and lack within and about you, is not the plan of the Divine, yet it is the number one disease that plagues 99% of human beings.

Poverty and lack within and about you, blinds you to the goodness and riches that your Creator has provided for you, in you, all around you. And wants you to have.

The Bible, the oldest and most read book in the world, is full of rich promises for our potential prosperity.

You need to be prosperous and well supplied because it is your divine heritage. Your Creator wants it to be so.

There is no reason to think of your prosperity as being separate and apart from your spiritual life. As a child of our DIVINE CREATOR, you are spiritual and, thus, intended to be naturally prosperous.

It is the will of your Creator that you are Absolutely Prosperous. If it were not so, you would not think or dream of experiencing prosperity. You would not be able to admire the prosperity that some have been able to create for themselves.

Do not make excuses for being in a state of lack.

You, too, can be Absolutely Prosperous and will be prosperous because it is your inherent right to be so.

Take your Divine Creator and Source of all good as He/She truly is: creative, rich, loving, kind, forgiving, understanding and generous.

I will share with you a technique that the Masters use to make and sustain direct contact with the Divine. You too can feel closer to, synchronized with, and commune with the Divine. Here you can be spiritually guided in all of your affairs whether it is Spiritual, financial or otherwise.

You can experience the pleasure of how quickly your life improves.

The Bible tells us "All things are yours". Believe it - they are yours.

Sacrifice, poverty, persecution and hard times are not necessary for spiritual growth or prosperity.

They are a blatant rejection of the Creator's good intended for you.

If you have been living your life in a belief that lack of good and prosperity are necessary states of being for whatever reason, and you have not been able to create for you, a prosperous life.

I encourage you to try something else now.

Your refusal to accept your divine inheritance of Absolute Prosperity, stagnates the PLAN of GOOD that our LOVING CREATOR has created for you.

Lack of Absolute Prosperity in and about YOU is not being spiritual.

You are a part of this universe. You are a link in the chain of GOOD, which is the plan of the Divine Creator.

History revealed that the teachings of the Bible became secularized during the early centuries after the death of Christ. This departure lead to many variations of the meaning of the DIVINE intended Good for us.

During the Middle Ages, in an effort to secure wealth and power for only a few, and to stave off rebellion, the Feudalists embraced and enhanced the secularized teachings of the Bible.

They taught the mass that "poverty and penance" were the only way to salvation. Millions accepted the idea that it was spiritual to be poor.

These same ideas about poverty as a spiritual virtue have persisted throughout the ages until today.

The truth is, our Creator's intent is for us to have and enjoy all that have been created. Therefore, lack is not a part of your Divine plan.

Accept your DIVINE heritage now and DECLARE:

I AM A DIVINE CREATION OF AN ALL-GOOD SOURCE, AND SO LIKE MY SOURCE, I AM NATURALY PROSPEROUS. I AM A CREATIVE, GOOD, KIND, HEALTHY, WEALTHY FORGIVING, AND LOVING DIVINE SOUL, AND I LOVE MYSELF.

I ACCEPT MY DIVINE HERITIGE OF ABSOLUTE PROSPERITY IN AND ABOUT ME. RIGHT HERE, RIGHT NOW. AND SO IT IS.

I am a part of one Creation, one Universal Consciousness and one Universe. I am a link in the chain of Good that is intended for all of us. That is the plan of our Divine Creator.

Our Divine Creator depends on you to co-create the intended GOOD, for ALL OF US. You cannot be of any good to yourself or to anyone else, being in a state of neediness.

THE DIVINE CAN AND WILL ONLY DO FOR YOU WHAT CAN BE DONE THROUGH YOU.

Make a bold decision to eradicate lack and poverty from every aspect of your life, and claim your Divine Heritage of Absolute Prosperity here and now.

This affirmation repeated several times daily can be very effective.

I RADIATE VIBRATIONS OF PROSPERITY AND WELL-BEING WHEREVER I AM EACH DAY, AND SO IN EVERY SECOND, OF EVERY MINUTE NOW AND FOR-EVER. I SHARE IN THE ABUN-DANT PROSPERITY THAT MY DIVINE CREATOR HAS CRE-ATED FOR AND GIVEN ME. I AM A MAGNET THAT PULLS ONLY THAT WHICH IS PEACE,

WEALTH, PREFECT HEALTH, WISDOM, JOY AND CONTENTMENT TO ME FROM MY CREATOR'S DIVINE SOURCE OF ABUNDANCE. HERE AND NOW. I ACCEPT MY DIVINE HERITAGE.

It is your desires, and your thoughts that will be given Divine Expression. Give thanks that Absolute Prosperity is your Divine Heritage; that your Creator's desire for you is infinite, constant, abundant GOODNESS; that the Divine's Will is for you to manifest all of the Good that there is in the Universe for you.

The consciousness of a human being is an energy field that is constantly being realized in our life experiences. We make real our life experiences what we think, say, feel and do.

The Human Being who does not realize a true sense of being in oneness with the DIVINE, will not experience prosperity in abundance, in any area or aspect of one's life, because this Being is not in sync with the Universal Consciousness. As a result, one's energy field does not vibrate harmoniously with the God-Mind or Universal Intelligence.

Whatever is manifested in one's life is directly the consequence of one's beliefs, desires, thoughts, feelings, and actions.

The Divine created Human Beings through the power of The Word.

"Be not deceived; God is not mocked: for whatever a man soweth, that shall he also reap."

Christ thought us; "For by thy word thou shall be justified and by thy word thou shall be condemned."

You are a creation of the Divine, and like the Divine. You Co-create with the Divine through your thoughts, words, deeds and actions.

I promised that I would share with you a technique of the Masters, so that you too can make direct sustained connection to the Universal Intelligence or Divine-Mind. Get synchronized, and be divinely guided to the infinite Good of Absolute Prosperity within and about you.

Permit yourself to be opened to the Universal Consciousness of Source, and be ready to live your life in ALL-GOOD consciousness of source and be ready to live your life, in a state of being Absolute Prosperity. Here and Now.

PART 3

MY INHERENT
MYSTICAL REALITY

CHAPTER 3
My Inherent Mystical Reality

You are a "Divine Soul" created by the Divine. Therefore, YOU, the Divine Soul, have the inherent right and ability to communicate directly with your Creator. Your intended natural state of being is to feel good, whole, happy and content within and about yourself.

Human Beings who have been able to create for them what may appear to some as miracles in their lives, consciously or unconsciously, live their lives in constant communion with the Divine. They live their lives in soul consciousness. In other words, their souls are the directing force in their lives. Their egos had very little to do with the prosperity that they have been able to materialize for themselves.

They came to the realization, that imbedded within their souls, was all of the knowledge that existed, and still does exists in the universe. With this realization, they made a conscious decision to purpose-fully live their lives, in the consciousness of their souls. One could say that they always acted on their gut feelings, and faith in some other source of higher intelligence.

Their successes are realized through the practice of what we call Mysticism.

You too must activate your natural state of being a "Metaphysician" if you are to manifest Absolute Prosperity as your life's reality.

Christ was the first and greatest Metaphysician who understood our possibilities.

When asked by his disciples, how could they not heal the sick, and perform the miracles he did Christ answered saying:

"If you have faith as a grain of mustard seed, ye shall say unto that mountain. Remove… and nothing shall be impossible unto you."

You must believe in, and have faith in your inherent Divine Mystical Powers to be able to create for you a life of Absolute Prosperity. It is yours for the taking, and no one, nothing, can take it away but you.

Do the Spiritual thing and TAKE ACTION NOW!

At one time or another we have all declared. "I wish that I followed my mind."

Why? If you had followed your mind, things would have gone right.

We have an inner voice, which is the voice of the Divine that is speaking to you through our soul. It is our Soul that leads us and directs us to prosperity.

The proven practice of mysticism will help you to live your life in DIVINE guidance, so that, you too, can follow your inner voice, which will eliminate confusion and lack in your life, so that you can manifest into reality the absolute prosperity that you desire.

What Is Mysticism

Mysticism is not card reading, crystal gazing or tealeaf reading. Mysticism is the highest quest of human's growth.

Mysticism is:

The discovery of your highest Self-Reality: such as the relationship of a human being's mind, and the mind of GOD or the Universal Consciousness.

It is the discovery of the Supreme Universal Intelligence, or the Divine-Mind that resides in the deeper levels of your mind.

It is to make direct contact with, and to live in

the knowledge of your Supreme Intelligence, or God-Mind.

To bring to the surface of your conscious mind, the infinite wisdom of the Divine-Mind, and manifest into existence, your Creativity, Attributes, and Power of the Universal Mind or Source for the purpose of improving your life.

Use INTUITIVE HSP (Higher Sensatory Perception) to successfully guide you in all that you do in your daily life.

Meditation is one of the modems that can be used by you, to effectively Synchronize your mind with the Universal Creative Intelligence, of your Divine Creator and source of all good, so that you can manifest for yourself the life that you desire - that which is intended by your Divine Creator to be yours.

Meditation

Meditation is the foundation of Practical Mysticism through which you can use the ultimate Power and Intelligence of the Universe that is within you, to manifest all the GOOD that you intend for yourself. Your Creator has given that to you and it is your Inherent Divine Right.

When Christ said, "go into your closet and pray," He meant go within yourself, into the privacy of your own mind, to purge your thoughts free from unsound perceptions.

Your mind is the only medium through which you can make direct contact with the DIVINE-MIND, or Universal Consciousness. Meditation serves to clear the clutter, and releases the mind to receive Divine impressions, that will lead one to a state of wholeness and wellbeing.

The practice of meditation requires that at least once each day, you go into your mind to release your everyday thoughts. In this way, the Conscious/ Unconsciousness of your God-mind, your inner voice or your sixth sense will surface and become apparent and dominant.

Through the practice of meditating for about 20 minutes daily you can strip away the layers of untruths, and make direct contact with the Divine Intelligence of the Universe, or God-Mind, through which the truth will be revealed to you on a spiritual level, and through which the good that you desire most, will be manifested as your life's reality.

The keys to achieving Absolute Prosperity in and about you are to know, believe in and to have confidence and faith in your true identity.

You are like your Creator. You are a very Wise, Powerful and Creative being - An ALL-GOOD "DIVINE SOUL," having a human experience.

You are filled with all the knowledge and power that exists in the Universe, The knowledge and power of your SOUL is absolutely, infinite and boundless.

Exercise your inherent mystical powers and become Absolutely Prosperous.

The Almighty tells us: " Be still and know that I am God."

Quiet the chattering that goes on in your mind by meditating, in order to create peace and space in your mind, so that you may hear and receive Divine guidance and experience Serenity in a State of being of well being.

Allow the conscious/unconsciousness of your mind to surface and be intuitively guided.

Meditate daily for 20 minutes to make direct contact with the Supreme Universal Intelligence, or God Mind.

Take this text with you wherever you go and read it. Repeat the affirmations as many times as possible throughout the course of the day.

This will help you to create your desired mental state.

Believe yourself to be at peace and poised each day in the calm self-assurance that the Universe prospers you.

Be in a state of expectancy. Be ready to receive. Listen to and follow Divine guidance. Take action in order to manifest that which is your Divine Heritage - a life of Absolute Prosperity.

Let your loving ALL-GOOD Creator be your guide.

Before going to sleep and upon awakening each day affirm:

MY MIND IS A PART OF THE INFINITE MIND OF GOD. I, THEREFORE, THINK OF MYSELF AS A PROSPEROUS SOUL. AS I DO, MY THOUGHTS TRAVEL INTO THE MIND OF GOD AND OPEN CHANNELS THROUGH WHICH MY NEEDS AND ALL THE GOOD THAT I DESIRE, FLOWS TO ME IN CONSTANT SUCCESSION.

MY MIND, THEREFORE, IS A MAGNET THAT DRAWS PROSPERITY TO ME. I DECLARE MY FATHER MOTHER GOD TO, LEAD AND DIRECT ME, BECAUSE YOU ARE THE SOURCE OF MY TRUE INTEL-

LIGENCE, AND THUS, THE SOURCE OF MY ABSOLUTE PROSPERITY. FOR THIS I GIVE THANKS THAT IT IS SO... AND SO IT IS!

Harmonize yourself with your Divine Source of ALL-GOOD. Be clear about what it is that you intend to manifest. Be sure that whatever you ask for is truly what you desire.

Your Creator is always in a state of creation and will create with you what it is that you intend to create for yourself.

The Divine is never imposing. That is why you have the freedom of thought. Do not wait on the Creator to do for you. You do. God will Co-Create with you and through you.

Do what is right spiritually. Take responsibility for your thoughts, deeds and actions, and make the right choices.

Find your true sense of being, your creative passion and Divine purpose through communicating with the Divine.

Ask the Divine for direction and answers to your questions. You will find that they will come almost instantaneously from anyone, thing or place.

Be aware. Be diligent. Be always in a state of expectancy.

Be very sure and clear about what it is that you desire. Believe that you deserve it; that it is your GOD-GIVEN right to have it; that you will have it "AND YOU WILL." It is your inherent right and so you MUST have it.

God's rich supply of GOOD intended for you is all around you and within you, as ideas, talents and abilities.

They are your dreams that are longing to be expressed through your creations.

Your mind is the connecting link to it. Your mental concepts, attitude and beliefs, are what you will manifest as your life's reality. Connect to, and synchronize your mind to your creator's rich supply of substance and good and manifest your intended desires of Absolute Prosperity to be your life's reality here and now.

Your Creator can and will only do for you, what can be done through you.

Take full responsibility.

Think Prosperity! It opens the way to prosperous results. Take action, and you will achieve all the good that you desire for yourself.

Spiritually eradicate " Fear" and "Guilt" from your mind and all aspects of your life. Go within your GOD-MIND. Tap into the Universal Intelligence, where you can and will get clarity and an understanding of unsound perception and thoughts.

Your Creator is forgiving and All-GOOD, and only creates that which is GOOD for you.

You are a Divine Soul created in the image and likeness of the Almighty.

You are like your Creator=very powerful and infinitely wise.

You Co-Create with Source and so it is possible for you to create everything that is GOOD for you, within and about you.

You must accept responsibility for your thoughts and actions and create the changes that you desire NOW, for the good of you, others, and the Universe.

Your thoughts, deeds, words and action make you what you are now and they will be your thoughts, deeds, words and actions that will make you what you are tomorrow and forever.

Nothing can stop you from manifesting into realty all good that you desire for yourself but you.

Boldly and confidently claim your heritage NOW!

I AM AN ALL- GOOD DIVINE SOUL WHO IS POWERFUL AND INFINITELY WISE.

MY THOUGHTS ARE THE THOUGHTS OF THE MIND OF GOD AND SO I CO-CRE-ATE WITH MY CREATOR, AND MANIFEST ONLY THAT WHICH IS GOOD FOR ME.

I AM FILLED WITH INFI-NITE, BOUNDLESS, POSSIBILI-TIES AND POWER TO CREATE ABSOLUTE PROSPERITY FOR ME HERE AND NOW. I LIVE IN ONENESS WITH THE RICH AND GOOD, SUPPLIES OF MY DIVINE CREATOR HERE AND NOW. AND SO IT IS. THANK YOU GOD.

"There is nothing new under the sun." This is true. The knowledge of my soul is boundless in its infinite wisdom, knowledge and understanding.

My Almighty Creator is always in a state of creation. If it were not so the universe would not be able to replenish itself; there would be no new land, human beings, grass, trees and birds.

I have done the spiritual thing and have taken responsibility for my thoughts, deeds and action, to CREATE for me, all the good that I truly desire.

And so I declare in the presence of the DIVINE SOUCE of all things:

MY CREATOR'S WILL FOR ME IS THAT I FEEL GOOD; THAT I EXPERIENCE PERFECT HEALTH, BE WHOLE; WITHIN AND ABOUT MYSELF, I AM WELL SUPPLIED WITII THE ALL THE ABDOUNDANCE CREATED FOR ME.

I LIVE EACH DAY OF MY LIFE, IN THE AWARENESS OF BEING IN SYNCRONIZED ONENESS, WITH THE GOD-MIND.

IN THIS STATE OF ONENESS WITH THE DIVINE, I PUT MY INHERENT POWERS OF POSSIBILITIES INTO ACTION.

MY THOUGHTS DEEDS AND

ACTIONS CONTINUOUSLY MANIFEST MY DIVINE GIFT OF ABSOLUTE PROSPERITY. THIS IS MY INHERENT, TRUE RIGHT OF PASSAGE. IT IS SO, AND SO IT IS. FOR THIS I GIVE THANKS. THANK YOU GOD.

Focus and act on the plan of GOOD that our loving Father/Mother has given you.

Treat others with the same love, and respect that you have for yourself.

Give back to the Source. You always have something that you can share. Keep in mind that, that which you sew you, will reap.

It would be useful to remember that we are all spiritual beings having a human experience. The only intent of the Soul is to manifest into reality that which is All-Good. The soul must emulate it's Source, and as the Soul progresses in the emulation of the Source, the human experiences change. So make allowance for yourself and others to grow.

You are a link in the chain of the Almighty Creator's intended GOOD WILL for ALL of US.

Start where you are NOW! Give no further thought to the fear, guilt or to the past. The past, is just that, the past.. Live every moment, of every day of your life, in the here and now.

Use the inherent powers of your soul to surgically eradicate fear, guilt and past experiences from your existence. They have already served to get you to this place.

Associate with like-minded people. Get a copy of this text into the hands of all of your family members, friends and close associates.

PART 4

BEGINNING
LIGHT MEDITATION

CHAPTER 4
BEGINNING LIGHT MEDITATION

- Select a time of day and place where you will not be disturbed.

- Wear loose clothing.

- Sit comfortably in an upright position; your back and spine should be as straight as possible.

- Close your eyes and relax your entire body slowly starting from your head to your toes.

- Visualize three brilliant globes of beautiful, bright white lights above your head.

- Pull each light one-by-one slowly into your body, starting from the top of your head to the sole of your feet..

- Let each light flow out of your body through your toes and the bottom of your feet.

This simple meditation should take about 20 minutes.

As you slowly open your eyes, stretch your hands upwards over your head and give thanks.

I have shared with you what I experienced and believe to be the PROVEN TRUTH.

It is your choice to create for yourself whatever it is that you desire to be your life's reality.

I BID YOU PEACE, AND ALL THE GOOD THAT YOU RIGHTFULLY DESERVE NOW AND FOREVER.

PART 5

WORLD

PRAYER

THE GREAT INVOCATION

From the point of Light within
The Mind of God
Let light stream forth into the
Human minds.
Let Light descend on Earth.

From the point of Love within
The Heart of God
Let love stream forth into the
Hearts of Human Beings
May Christ return to Earth.

From the centre where the Will
of God is known
Let purpose guide the little wills
of all Human Beings

The purpose, which the Masters
know and serve.

From the centre that we call the
Human Race
Let the Plan of Love and Light
work out
And may it seal the door where
Evil dwells.

Let Light and Love and Power
restore the Plan on Earth.